Scary Creatures
KILLER WHALES

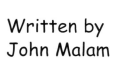

Written by
John Malam

Created and designed
by David Salariya

FRANKLIN WATTS
An Imprint of Scholastic Inc.
NEW YORK • TORONTO • LONDON • AUCKLAND • SYDNEY
MEXICO CITY • NEW DELHI • HONG KONG
DANBURY, CONNECTICUT

Author:

John Malam studied ancient history and archeology at the University of Birmingham, England, after which he worked as an archeologist at the Ironbridge Gorge Museum in Shropshire. He is now an author specializing in nonfiction books for children on a wide range of subjects. He lives in Cheshire with his wife and their two young children. Website: www.johnmalam.co.uk

Artists:

John Francis
Robert Morton
Mark Bergin
Carolyn Scrace
Richard Coombes

Series Creator:

David Salariya was born in Dundee, Scotland. In 1989 he established The Salariya Book Company. He has illustrated a wide range of books and has created many new series for publishers in the U.K. and overseas. He lives in Brighton, England, with his wife, illustrator Shirley Willis, and their son.

Editor: Stephen Haynes

Editorial Assistants:
Rob Walker, Tanya Kant

Picture Research:
Mark Bergin, Carolyn Franklin

Photo Credits:

t=top, b=bottom

Galina Barskaya/Fotolia: 27
Mark Bergin: 11, 18, 24
Cadmium: 12b
Lars Christensen/Fotolia: 13
Corel: 21
Nolie Gumapac/Fotolia: 25
Thomas Kitchin & Victoria Hurst/NHPA: 22
Xavier Marchant/Fotolia: 23
Mountain High Maps/© 1993 Digital
   Wisdom Inc.: 28–29
philippev/Fotolia: 26

PAPER FROM
SUSTAINABLE
FORESTS

Created, designed, and produced by
The Salariya Book Company Ltd
Book House
25 Marlborough Place
Brighton BN1 1UB

A CIP catalog record for this title is available from the Library of Congress.

ISBN-13: 978-0-531-20447-4 (Lib. Bdg.)
        978-0-531-21006-2 (Pbk.)
ISBN-10: 0-531-20447-2 (Lib. Bdg.)
        0-531-21006-5 (Pbk.)

Published in the United States by Franklin Watts
An Imprint of Scholastic Inc.
557 Broadway
New York, NY 10012

Printed in China

Killer whale toying with a sea lion

Contents

Are Killer Whales Fish?

Killer whales look like fish. Like fish, they live in the sea, have fins and flippers, and have **streamlined** bodies. But killer whales are not fish! They are **mammals**—just like cats, rabbits, and humans. Like all mammals, they are warm-blooded, have lungs that breathe air, and give birth to live babies that drink milk from their mothers.

Whales, dolphins, and porpoises belong to a group of sea mammals called **cetaceans** (from an ancient Greek word meaning "sea monsters"). The killer whale is the largest of the dolphins.

X-Ray Vision

Hold the next page up to the light and see what's inside a killer whale.

See what's inside

Male killer whale
23 feet (7 m) long

Hector's dolphin
5 feet (1.5 m)

Blue whale
100 feet (30 m)

Adult human
5-6 feet
(1.5-1.8 m)

A killer whale attacks a sea lion, tossing it out of the water before catching it in its mouth.

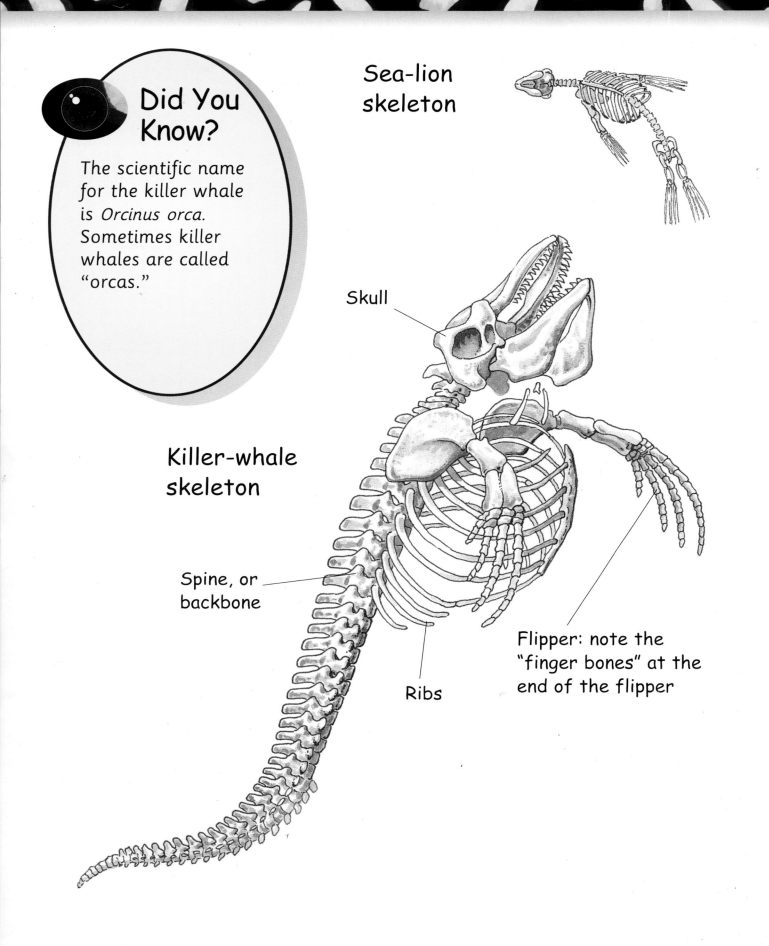

Sea-lion skeleton

Killer-whale skeleton

Skull

Spine, or backbone

Ribs

Flipper: note the "finger bones" at the end of the flipper

What Do Killer Whales Eat?

Killer whales eat many animals, including other whales. They are the ocean's top **predator**. Adults eat about 550 pounds (250 kg) of food every day—and not all of it comes from the sea. For example, they will snatch sea birds that settle on the water and grab seals off beaches.

Did You Know?

Killer whales are known to eat land animals, such as moose and caribou (reindeer). The whales attack these animals as they swim across sea channels, moving from one feeding ground to another.

Gray whale calf

Sea birds

Squid

Fish

Penguin

Sea turtle

Seal

Manatee

Dolphin

Killer whales are not picky eaters. Their diet ranges from soft squid to tough turtles, small fish to giant whales. Scientists have either seen killer whales eating these animals, or found their remains inside the killer whales' stomachs. There's good news for humans—killer whales don't eat us!

How Big Is a Killer Whale?

Male killer whales are bigger than females. Adult males grow to about 23 feet (7 m) long and weigh 5 tons, while females reach about 20 feet (6 m) and 4 tons. Both males and females take around 10 years to grow into adults. Killer whales may be big, but many whales are bigger—the massive blue whale can be up to 100 feet (30 m) long.

Killer-whale tooth

A killer whale's teeth are sharp and pointed and curve backward into its mouth. This is the best shape for holding onto and tearing at **prey**.

Flukes

Did You Know?

An adult killer whale has between 40 and 56 teeth, each of which is about 3 inches (7.5 cm) long.

Young whale (calf)

Adult female (cow)

Male killer whales are called **bulls**, females are **cows**, and young whales are **calves**.

Dorsal fin

Gray saddle-patch marking

Adult male (bull)

The **saddle-patch** marking behind the dorsal fin is different on every whale—just as all humans have different fingerprints.

Blowhole

Eye

Eye patch

Pectoral fin or flipper

Males and females can be told apart by the shape of their **dorsal** (back) **fins**. Male dorsals grow to 6 feet (1.8 m), and are upright. Female dorsals are smaller, at about 4 feet (1.2 m), and they usually curve backward.

Female

Male

How Fast Is a Killer Whale?

Killer whales are the fastest members of the whale family, with a top speed of about 30 miles (48 km) per hour. Their "cruising speed" is about 6 miles (10 km) per hour. Their bodies are streamlined, like torpedoes. A smooth shape helps them move more easily through the water.

Did You Know?

Killer whales are not the fastest animals in the sea—the sailfish swims in bursts of up to 70 miles (113 km) per hour. Human swimmers can only manage a top speed of about 5 miles (8 km) per hour.

A killer whale swims by moving its powerful tail up and down through the water. The harder it "beats" its tail, the faster it swims. It changes direction by moving its pectoral fins.

Pectoral fins

Lobtailing (above) is when a killer whale lifts its tail clear out of the water, then slaps it down to make a loud splash. It does this when hunting, to force fish to swim toward others in its group.

Sometimes killer whales lie on their sides and splash the water surface with their pectoral fins. This is called **flippering**. Perhaps they do this to send signals to other killer whales.

Killer whales are sociable animals. Sometimes they leap out of the water, in a display to others in their **pod** (family group). This is called **breaching**.

How Long Can a Killer Whale Hold Its Breath?

Killer whales are air-breathing animals and come to the surface to fill their lungs. A killer whale breathes through a blowhole at the top of its head. When it dives, it closes its blowhole and holds its breath. Adults usually stay underwater for about 5 minutes. But on deep dives, down to 100 feet (30 m), they can hold their breath for as long as 15 minutes.

A killer whale breathes out stale air through its blowhole, making a **spout** of water droplets. Then it breathes in to refill its lungs with air.

Their lungs now filled with air, a pair of killer whales prepare to dive below the surface, where they will hunt for food. The male has the tall, upright dorsal fin; the female has the shorter, curved fin.

Baby killer whales are born underwater. The first thing they do is swim to the surface to fill their lungs with air. As they swim up, they keep their blowholes tightly closed.

Killer whales have black backs and white bellies. These are camouflage colors that help to break up the whale's outline, making it harder for prey animals to spot the whale as it moves toward them.

How Do Killer Whales Hunt?

Killer whales hunt in family groups or pods. They are known as the "wolves of the sea," because wolves also hunt in packs. To find prey, the whales make clicking sounds, then listen for echoes as the clicks bounce off fish, seals, and other animals. They can tell from the echoes what kind of prey it is. When the whales have located prey, they swim around it, herding it into a small circle. This makes it easier to attack.

Did You Know?

In the Antarctic, pods of killer whales knock sleeping seals and penguins off ice sheets, and then catch them as they fall into the sea.

Finding prey by sound is called **echolocation**. It means that killer whales don't need to see their prey. That's useful at night and in deep or murky water.

Killer whales on the hunt

Outgoing clicks

Incoming echoes

School of fish

Killer-whale skin is smooth and rubbery. It is coated in oil, which helps the killer whale slide quickly through the water. Unlike land mammals, whales do not have hair or fur. Instead, just under the skin is a thick layer of fat called **blubber**. The blubber layer helps to keep heat in, even in freezing polar waters.

The pointed teeth of a killer whale can easily puncture the skin of a seal. Because the teeth point backward, the seal finds it hard to free itself from the whale's grip. The killer whale might "play" with the seal after it kills it, using its mighty tail like a bat to knock its body high into the air. The whale then eats the seal.

Dorsal fin

Blowhole

Blubber

Muscle

Common seal (harbor seal)

How Long Does a Killer Whale Live?

A baby killer whale is inside its mother's body for about 15 months before it is born. If it survives its first few months, it may have a long life ahead of it. Females often live for 80 to 90 years. Males live about 50 years.

When a calf is born, it comes out tail first. It can weigh up to 450 pounds (200 kg) and measure about 8 feet (2.5 m) long. Within seconds, its mother guides it to the surface with her flippers and it takes its first breath of air. After half an hour, the baby can swim unaided.

Killer-whale calf

The mother feeds her calf with milk, which she squirts into its mouth. The calf stays close to its mother, always swimming close by her side. When it is about two years old, it starts to move away and hunt for solid food with the rest of the pod.

Female killer whale

Who Lives in a Killer-Whale Family?

Killer whales live their whole lives in a family group or pod. It's made up of mothers and their calves. As mothers give birth to new calves, these become half brothers and half sisters to the older calves. The fathers come from a different pod, where they live with their mothers.

X-Ray Vision

Hold the next page up to the light and see what's under the water.

See what's inside

Orca pod

A pod has 10 to 20 whales in it, headed by a senior female.

Killer whales can "stand" on their tails, poking their heads above the surface of the water. This is called **spyhopping**. Killer whales spyhop when they want to see what's above the water.

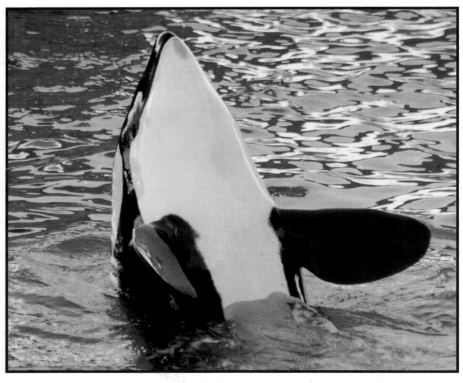

Spyhopping

Several generations of a killer-whale family live together—children, parents, grandparents, and even great-grandparents.

Who Studies Killer Whales?

The best place to study killer whales is in the wild, where they can be seen behaving naturally. Scientists spend years studying individuals and pods, watching them from boats, swimming alongside them, and following their travels with the help of space satellites. They also listen to and record their clicks and calls. All of this is important work that helps us to learn about the lives of these wonderful whales.

Scientists can keep track of a killer whale by fitting it with a radio transmitter. Satellites can then record its location.

Suction cups

Antenna

Radio transmitter

Individual killer whales can be recognized by their dorsal fins. Each fin is shaped slightly differently and may have identifying nicks along its edges.

What Is Whale Watching?

When tourists travel out to sea to look at whales, they are whale watching. Whale watchers go out in boats big and small, from rubber rafts with just four or five people to large boats carrying hundreds of people. Sometimes the whales are nowhere to be seen—but tourists who do see killer whales in the wild always say how exciting it is to watch them. If the whales spyhop around the boats, they are people watching!

Killer whales seem to enjoy being close to humans. They put on displays of breaching, lobtailing, flippering, spyhopping, and spouting.

Tongue

A killer whale's tongue is short and strong and has a movable tip. This tip pushes food toward the whale's throat.

Are Killer Whales in Danger?

Killer whales have never been hunted in large numbers by whalers, and there could be as many as 100,000 of them in the sea. But pollution puts them at risk, and they sometimes get trapped in fishing nets. In some places fishermen have used guns and explosives to wipe out entire pods, blaming the killer whales for eating too much fish.

Killer whales have been kept in captivity since the 1960s. Nearly all of them have been taken from the wild; very few have been born in zoos or water parks. A killer whale taken from the sea loses contact with its pod, which is harmful for both the whale and its family group.

Look at the dorsal fin on this killer whale. Can you see how it's bent over? It should be upright. When a dorsal fin collapses like this, it shows the killer whale is stressed and unhappy. A killer whale taken from the sea will live only about five years in captivity.

Did You Know?

Keiko was a killer whale caught near Iceland in 1979. He was put on show in Iceland, Canada, and Mexico. In 1993 he starred in the film *Free Willy*. In 2002 he was released into the sea, but he no longer knew how to survive in the wild and died the following year.

What do you think?

About 150 killer whales have been taken out of the wild and then kept in tanks or pools, where they are made to perform for audiences. Do you think it is right to do this?

25

How Does Pollution Harm Killer Whales?

Humans are the worst enemies of killer whales. This is not because killer whales are hunted or captured, but because their natural **habitat** is being poisoned by toxins (toxic chemicals). Some toxins are deliberately dumped at sea, but others get there by accident. Although seawater dilutes the toxins and spreads them far and wide, they still find their way into the bodies of killer whales. Today, killer whales are the world's most contaminated whales.

Oil spilled accidentally from ships can be just as dangerous to sea creatures as poisons that are dumped on purpose. Other toxins may be washed into the sea from streams and rivers.

Once the toxins are in the sea, there is no way to take them out. They enter the food chain and eventually end up inside killer whales.

Did You Know?

Killer-whale mothers with toxins in their bodies can pass the poisons to their young. While the babies are inside their mothers, toxins pass into them through the bloodstream. After they are born, toxins are passed to the young through their mothers' milk. This makes them more vulnerable to disease.

How does a food chain work?

Animals eat plants or other animals, and then they themselves get eaten by something else. This is a food chain. At the bottom of the chain is plankton—a mass of tiny plants and animals that drift in the sea. Plankton absorbs the toxins that are in the water. Then the plankton is eaten by shrimp-like creatures called krill, and the toxins pass into their bodies. When krill are eaten by squids, seals, penguins, and other animals, the toxins are passed on. At the top of the food chain are killer whales. Toxins enter their bodies when they eat squids, seals, and penguins.

Why are toxins dumped at sea?

Toxins are often dumped at sea because this is cheaper than disposing of them safely on land. Some people think that poisoning the sea does not matter because humans do not live there. Others think you don't need to worry about things you can't see. But the sea and its creatures are part of our own food chain as well.

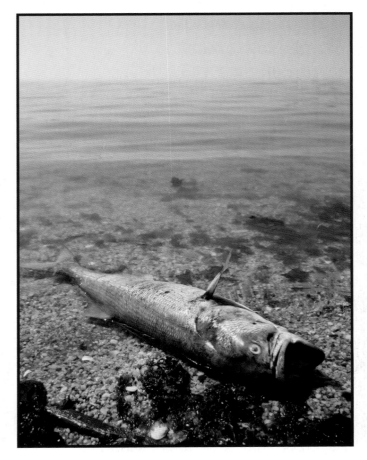

Cetaceans Around the World

Whales, dolphins, and porpoises are found in all the world's oceans and seas. Some are long-distance travelers, while others spend their whole lives in one part of the world.

Humpback whale
Found: Most oceans
Length: 43 feet (13 m)
Weight: 40 tons

Minke whale
Found: Most oceans
Length: 26 feet (8 m)
Weight: 10 tons

Sperm whale
Found: Most oceans
Length: 59 feet (18 m)
Weight: 45 tons

North America

Atlantic Ocean

Pacific Ocean

South America

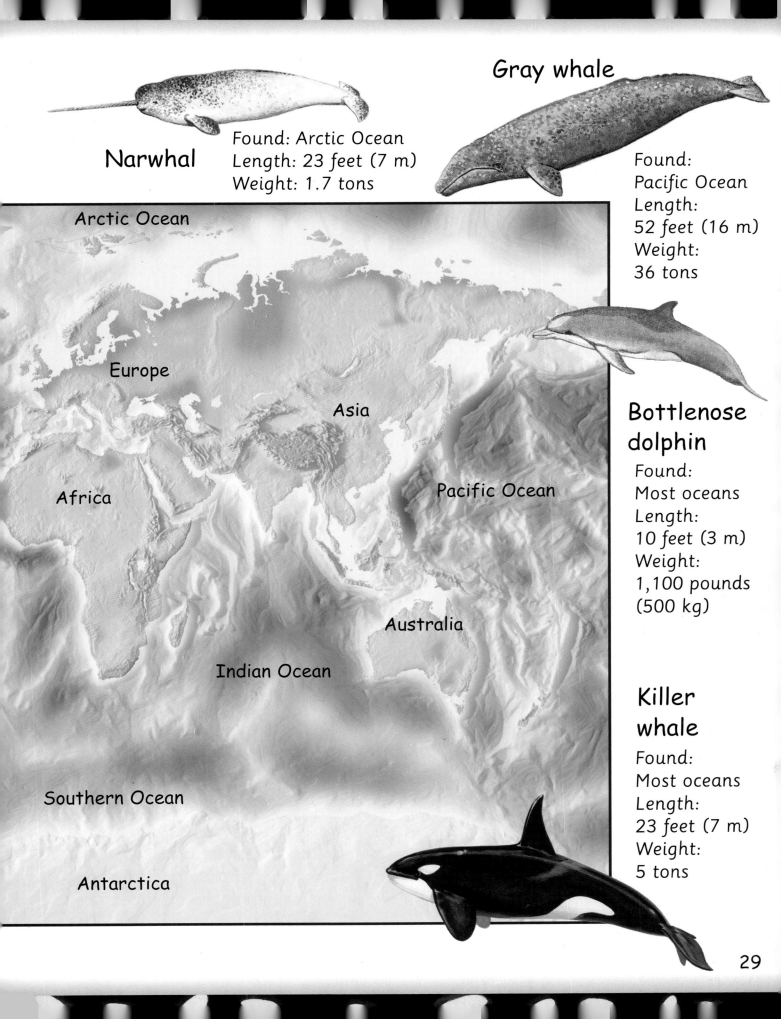

Narwhal
Found: Arctic Ocean
Length: 23 feet (7 m)
Weight: 1.7 tons

Gray whale
Found:
Pacific Ocean
Length:
52 feet (16 m)
Weight:
36 tons

Bottlenose
dolphin
Found:
Most oceans
Length:
10 feet (3 m)
Weight:
1,100 pounds
(500 kg)

Killer
whale
Found:
Most oceans
Length:
23 feet (7 m)
Weight:
5 tons

Arctic Ocean

Europe

Asia

Africa

Pacific Ocean

Australia

Indian Ocean

Southern Ocean

Antarctica

Killer-Whale Facts

Most scientists believe that there is only one species of killer whale, but there are different groups. American and Canadian scientists have found three different groups in the Pacific Ocean.

Resident killer whales live near the coast and feed mainly on fish.

Transient killer whales travel more and feed mainly on marine mammals such as seals. Sometimes they will refuse to eat fish, even when there is nothing else to eat.

Offshore killer whales live far from land. They eat fish as resident whales do, but they travel in larger pods.

Killer whales were given their name long ago by whale hunters who saw them feeding on the bodies of dead whales. They called them "whale killers," but over time the name has been switched around to become "killer whales."

When a killer whale closes its mouth, its top and bottom teeth lock together. This helps the killer whale grip large prey and tear it into smaller pieces for easier swallowing.

In the early 1970s the United States Navy trained killer whales to dive to the seabed to recover lost objects such as torpedoes. They went as deep as 850 feet (260 m).

Each pod of killer whales has its own "language" of clicks. This helps the whales to keep in touch with their pod and not wander off to another group.

Male killer whales have a growth spurt when they are about 15 years old. This period, called "sprouting," is when their dorsal fins grow to adult size.

Glossary

beach rubbing Rubbing the body against pebbles in shallow water.

blowhole The breathing hole on top of a whale's head.

blubber The thick layer of fat just under a whale's skin.

breaching Leaping out of the water, then landing with a splash.

bull An adult male killer whale.

calf A young whale.

captivity The state of living in a human-made environment, such as a zoo.

cetaceans The group of animals to which whales, dolphins, and porpoises belong. The word means "sea monsters."

cow An adult female killer whale.

dorsal fin The fin on the back of a whale or fish.

echolocation Making sounds and listening to the returning echoes. Whales and bats use this to find food and to navigate.

flippering Slapping a flipper onto the surface of the water.

flukes The two fins of a whale's tail.

habitat The natural environment in which a plant or animal lives.

lobtailing Slapping the tail onto the surface of the water.

mammal An animal that has lungs that breathe air, is warm-blooded, gives birth to live babies, and feeds them on mother's milk.

pectoral fins Front fins or flippers.

pod A family of whales that live together.

predator An animal that hunts and kills other animals for food.

prey An animal that is eaten or hunted by a predator.

saddle patch A light-colored patch behind the dorsal fin of a killer whale.

spout A misty spray of stale air blown out through the blowhole.

spyhopping Lifting the head out of the water to have a look around.

streamlined Having a smooth shape that can move through air or water.

Index